Called to Endure With Joy!

OVERCOMING CRISIS

God's Way

How to Allow Christ Jesus to "Work it Out!" For You!

———— † ————

BY DR. RUTH TANYI

CONTENTS

PREFACE

LED BY GOD

It was the week of July 20th, 2020, and I was finishing a sermon for our Ministry's third annual Women's Conference titled, "Are You Still Doubting?". This conference was scheduled for July 25th, 2020. Due to the COVID-19 California State Law prohibiting various public gatherings, for the first time ever in our Ministry, we would be live streaming our Women's conference. Then, about three days before the conference, I started to discern in my spirit, this title: **"Called to Endure with Joy"**. The following day, I continued to discern that title in my spirit. After much prayer, I quickly realized that God was leading me to change the message for that conference. Again with much prayer, I discerned a confirmation in my spirit about changing my message. At this point, I only had about one day to prepare a new message titled exactly as I was led by God: *Called to Endure with Joy!*

It was challenging to prepare a message within a 24-hour period to be delivered in front of a Live-Stream audience for the first time. But with God, nothing is impossible (Luke 1:37; NKJV)! The day of the conference came, and whoa!—Glory to God! The response after the conference was a solid confirmation that it was indeed God. My obedience to change the message produced "much fruit" and continues to do so for God's Kingdom. Even though it was our first Live- Streamed event, and with only a few days to advertise the conference, we had about 150 people tune in to watch the live broadcast. Then, within just a few weeks of the broadcast, close to 800 people watched the replay from our Facebook page and YouTube channel combined, and more continue to watch today.

Additionally, we continue to receive dozens of testimonials from viewers telling us of how the teaching has been a "Game Changer" for them, empowering them to overcome this challenging COVID-19 season, and has equipped them with practical ways to overcome hardships from a Godly perspective.

I am believing God that hundreds and thousands more individuals will continue to watch that video teaching from our YouTube channel and Facebook page and be transformed.

Then, just when I thought I was through with the topic, about 3 weeks after the conference, I discerned again, very clearly in my spirit that the Lord was leading me to write this book, in order to reach a different type of audience with the same message taught on that July 25th, 2020 conference. And again in obedience, I decided to adhere to the Lord's directions.

Just as the video teaching continues to transform the lives of hundreds of individuals, I believe that God has the best plans for you, dear reader. I am trusting God that He will use the teachings in this book to speak to your heart, revealing simple, yet practical ways that will enable you to overcome your daily challenges and triumph in every area of life. **The teachings in this book will equip you with timeless principles from God's Word that will enable you to triumph, not just during this COVID-19 Pandemic, but beyond.**

Personally, I have practiced all of the principles I will teach in this book, so I know they work 100%. Some of you might have read my testimonial book of how I endured severe pain, suffering, and hardship, and eventually received my healing from the Lord from Metastasis Colon Cancer almost 12 years ago. So I know firsthand what pain and suffering is like, and I know that God's Word is the only solution to overcoming various calamities that may befall us in this life. Unfortunately, since we live in a Fallen World, until the second coming of our Lord Jesus Christ, we will encounter various trials, tribulations, hardships, pains, sorrows, etc. **Hence, this book serves as an excellent resource in preparing you to approach the calamities of life from a Godly perspective.** Since God is "no respecter of persons" (Acts 10:34; Romans 2:11), meaning He is impartial, as you practice the principles I will teach in this book, you will endure with joy and overcome, just as I did fighting Cancer.

Lastly, I intentionally wrote this book in a simple and practical manner so that it can be read through in one-seating. Because this is a Biblically-based teaching book, I recommend that you have a Bible in hand as you read, or at the very least, write down the Scriptures referenced in this book, so you can meditate on them later on.

In the name of Jesus, I pray that your hearts are open to receive whatever God wants to do in your life as you study this book. May God's peace and presence comfort you always, in Jesus name, Amen

Sincerely,

Dr Tanyi

August, 2020

CHAPTER 1

GOD IS NOT RESPONSIBLE

Every good and perfect gift is from above, coming down from the Father of the heavenly lights, who does not change like shifting shadows (James 1:17; New International Version, NIV).

I want to start this book by categorically explaining that God is not responsible for all of the pains, sufferings, calamities, etc., we are experiencing today. As the Scripture above correctly stated, The God of the Bible, the Only True Living God is a good, good Father, and there is no evil or deceit in Him (James 1:17). The Bible teaches that this current earth is not God's best. This is a Fallen World, brought about because of Adam and Eve's willful disobedience of God's instructions as recorded in Genesis chapter three.

When Adam and Eve willfully sinned against God and ate out of the forbidden tree, Sin and death entered into God's perfect creation (Romans 5:12). As a result, God, in His perfect justice pronounced judgment and cursed the soil (See Genesis Chapter 3). Ever since then, all kinds of calamities, diseases, hardships, pains, sorrows, etc., have been plaguing Mankind. This, however, was not God's original plan for His creation. Unfortunately, Satan, the Evil One, is taking advantage of this Fallen World and Mankind's Fallen Nature, and is deceiving people, leading millions to make wrong decisions thereby hurting themselves, others, and society at large. Satan has even deceived millions of people to blame God for their calamities in this life— that is a lie!—God is a good, good Father!

Because we live in a Fallen World, sadly, "bad things continue to happen to good people". Hence, it goes without saying, that sooner or later, if you live long enough, you will experience some kind of a trial, hardship, heartache, calamity, disease, etc, which will test your faith in God. As an example, who would have known that the COVID-19 Pandemic would happen in the year 2020 and "shake" the core beliefs of millions of people? Just like the COVID-19 Pandemic crisis, many of you reading this book are probably experiencing various hardships you never could have imagined – it could be a terminal diagnosis, a wayward child, an unexpected divorce, a failed business and/or bankruptcy, an unexpected death of a loved one, etc. Regardless of the calamity, as Christians, we have the firm assurance and hope that God is always with us, helping us through it all (Psalm 46:1).

> *If you are unsure, a Christian is anyone who genuinely believes in his or her heart, and has openly declared that the Lord Jesus Christ is the Messiah.*

As the Messiah, only the Lord Jesus is the Savior of Mankind from that Sinful Nature each human being inherits at the time of his or her birth into this world, because of that Sin committed by Adam and Eve as recorded in Genesis chapter 3. Once a confession of faith in Christ is declared, such a person is instantly considered saved (i.e., redeemed from that Sinful Nature) (Romans 10:9). Take note that becoming a Christian (i.e., a follower of Jesus Christ) is purely based on God's grace because of the Lord Jesus' death, burial, and resurrection over 2000 years ago, and the only response required from you is to accept this Gospel Message (i.e., good news) by faith (Ephesians 2:8-9).

As Christians therefore, no matter how severe our hardships and various calamities might be, we do not have to end up in despair, or rely on alcohol, sex, drugs, etc., to numb the pain and suffering; these substances never work anyway, they will only lead to worsening of the problem. **Our hope in God through Christ and the power from the Holy Spirit is our anchor to enable us to withstand any hardship in this Fallen World** (Hebrews 6:18-19). God is your friend, dear brethren in

Christ! God is not to be blamed! He desires to help you through it all, you can trust Him!

GOD IS NOT TO BE BLAMED!

Unfortunately, many individuals are incorrectly blaming God for all of the calamities, heartaches and various pains and sufferings they are experiencing. But God is not to be blamed! Rather, Adam and Eve are to be blamed as already explained. Much worse, your enemy, Satan, has deceived millions of people into thinking that God is responsible for their problems. Think about this for a minute: **if Satan can deceive you that God is responsible for your calamities, it will cause you to become passive, not seeking help from God, right?**

If you do not seek God's help, which is the only source for any true resolution of your calamity, Satan will win the "battle" and your suffering deepens. For the Christian, although Satan might win the "battle", he can never win the "war" because he is a defeated foe who already lost the "war" when Jesus rose from the dead (See Matthew 28). So do not be deceived, God is on your side, wanting to help you, so trust Him through whatever hardships you are going through right now.

Also, know that your pains, sufferings, trials, hardships, etc., do not surprise God. Most importantly—He is not punishing you, nor does He use pain and suffering to teach you a lesson, as some people incorrectly teach.

The Bible is very clear that God uses His Word primarily to correct us (2 Timothy 3:16), nothing else! Nonetheless, God can use our pains, sufferings, calamities, etc., to transform our lives for the better, if we allow Him to (Romans 8:28-29). This is why many people erroneously teach that God permitted the calamity in their lives in order to glorify Himself —False!

Now, the Bible teaches about Godly sorrow that leads to

repentance which will glorify God, and how God can use our daily circumstances in order to test and strengthen us (Deuteronomy 8:2; 2 Corinthians 7:10). The topic of God testing us is beyond the scope of this book. But suffice to say that, these are biblical truths, which unfortunately some people have misunderstood and concluded that God allows various pains, sufferings and calamities, etc., to "teach us a lesson". **This notion is unscriptural and FALSE, and is defaming to God's Holy character. If you maintain such a false notion, you would be saying that God leads us to sin and disobedience in order to use that to "teach us a lesson". This kind of erroneous thinking is detrimental to your relationship with God; your spiritual health; and is confusing and illogical; because the Bible teaches that God cannot lead us to sin and temptation** (James 1:13-15).

Satan, the father and author of lies and confusion is the one who leads people into temptations, and not God (John 8:44). Plus, the Lord Jesus teaches that it is Satan's will for us to suffer (John 10:10). Hence, in order for Satan to fulfill His will in your life, which only produces pain and suffering, he has to tempt you to sin and to disobey God.

Some of you may be discouraged because it appears as if there is so much pain and suffering in this world. Well, due to space limitation in this book, I cannot provide an in-depth answer to this common perspective. But here is the biblical response to this perspective, and this is the bottom line: **God has given each of us a Free Will, and unfortunately, people make poor choices, and as such have allowed the Evil One, Satan, an inroad into their lives, thus causing all sorts of pain and suffering.** Others are openly disobeying God, living and practicing sin, as such, they are dealing with the consequences of their actions—disobedience and living in sin always lead to severe consequences.

THE LAW OF REAPING AND SOWING

The Bible teaches that, just because God is love in His nature does not mean that He automatically absolves us from the consequences of poor choices or sin. You know why? Because God is also Just! **We serve a God that will always uphold Justice! If He were to absolve us from all of the consequences of our actions, that would not be Justice, right?** The pain and suffering that usually follows after our poor choices is simply the manifestation of God's Law of reaping and sowing. Several Scriptures teach this principle, here is one of them, *Do not be deceived: God cannot be mocked. A man reaps what he sows. Whoever sows to please their flesh, from the flesh will reap destruction; whoever sows to please the Spirit, from the Spirit will reap eternal life* (Galatians 6:7-8; emphasis author's).

Friend, God is not punishing people; rather, some people are just experiencing the sowing and reaping effects from their actions. But as you genuinely repent and stop disobeying God, in His mercy, He will accept your repentance, and will enable you to change your behaviors, as you allow Him to. Nevertheless, you will still have to deal with the pains, sufferings, hardships, etc., associated with the sin, disobedience, or wrong decisions, but God is always available to help you to endure the painful consequences.

GODLY PEOPLE EQUALLY SUFFER

But then, there are several others who are experiencing intense pain and suffering because of their righteousness (i.e., persecution) (Matthew 5:10-12). Still, there are many others who are not disobeying God nor practicing sin, yet, they are suffering from various calamities for reasons we do not quite understand. Personally, when I was diagnosed with Metastasis Colon Cancer, I could not fathom how and why because I was in perfect health and had no personal or family history of any type of Cancer, plus I was not living in sin.

The doctors considered my diagnosis and prognosis as unique because I did not fit into the pattern of a "typical" patient with Metastasis Colon Cancer. But when after much struggling I finally accepted the truth that we live in a Fallen World, and

God was not responsible for the cancer that attacked my body, I was able to seek His help, and as such endured with joy and received my healing. You can obtain the details of that cancer journey from my testimonial book titled: **Healed By the Stripes of Jesus! My Story! My Miracle! How I overcame Metastasis Colon Cancer! You can Be Healed Too!**

GOD IS THE ONLY SOURCE OF TRUE HOPE

Friend, regardless of the reason(s) for your suffering, here is the biblical response: **God, in His infinite wisdom, knew that Mankind would encounter various trials, tribulations, calamities, hardships, etc., in this Fallen Word. Hence, in His unfathomable love and grace, He has blessed us with the gift of Salvation through Jesus Christ; the presence of the Holy Spirit and His Revealed Word, so as to enable us to endure with joy.** Thus, instead of blaming God or allowing Satan to deceive you, how about you start, today, by meditating on the firm hope and confidence you have in the Triune God to enable you to endure with joy and overcome. In fact, God's Word teaches that we, as Christians, are called to endure with joy. Proceed now to the next chapter to learn more.

IN CONCLUSION

ɞ God is not responsible for all of the hardships people encounter in this world—that original Sin committed by Adam and Eve is;

ɞ Millions of people are experiencing various pains and sufferings because of their poor choices, others are due to reasons we do not know;

ɞ God does not punish us with pain and suffering to "teach us a lesson". Rather, He uses His Word to correct us, if we choose to obey;

ɞ God has offered Mankind the solution to our problems: Salvation through Jesus Christ; the empowerment from the Holy Spirit, and His Revealed Word.

ADDITIONAL RESOURCES

Available @: www.DrRuthTanyi.org/bookstore OR www.DrRuthHealingTestimony.com

1. Healed By the Stripes of Jesus! My Story! My Miracle! How I overcame Metastasis Colon Cancer! You can Be Healed Too!

2. **Also Available in Audio CD & USB Formats:** Healed By the Stripes of Jesus! My Story! My Miracle! How I overcame Metastasis Colon Cancer! You can Be Healed Too!

....

CHAPTER 2

CHRISTIANS ARE CALLED TO ENDURE WITH JOY

Therefore we do not lose heart. Though outwardly we are wasting away, yet inwardly we are being renewed day by day. For our light and momentary troubles are achieving for us an eternal glory that far outweighs them all. So we fix our eyes not on what is seen, but on what is unseen, since what is seen is temporary, but what is unseen is eternal (2 Corinthians 4:16-18; New International Version, NIV)

As Christians, we have been baptized by the Holy Spirit into the "Body of Christ", and by faith we have inherited a brand-new nature (2 Corinthians 5:17). This current earth is not our home. We are pilgrims, heading to our final destination which is heaven, in the presence of the Triune God throughout all eternity (Hebrews 11:13). **Hence, as the Scripture above teaches, all of our pains and sufferings are temporal — they will come to pass! In my view, this biblical truth in and of itself is a faith builder, enabling us to endure with joy as we struggle to maintain a Godly perspective during crisis.**

Also, as Christians, we have been sealed (i.e., being preserved for God's use) by the Holy Spirit (Ephesians 1:13), and the Triune God now lives on the inside of us! Hallelujah! We are therefore God's co-workers through Christ Jesus (Ephesians 2:10), and through the empowerment from the Holy Spirit, God wants us to serve Him in diverse ways in order to advance His Kingdom here on the earth. We are called, meaning, God has preordained certain tasks for us to accomplish on the earth. As an example, we are called by God collectively as a Church and as individuals to: (1) serve Him through our local churches, various ministries and outreaches as the opportunities become available;(2) proclaim the Gospel message; (3) serve the poor; (4) treat others with agape (unconditional) love; (5) forgive others;

(6) give financially into His work; etc (See Ephesians 4:30-34; Colossians 3:13).

While the above "callings" are popularly known and accepted by many Christians, in my experience, there is one calling that is not too popular—the call to endure hardships and various trials in our journey as Christians. According to the Marian-Webster dictionary, one description/definition of the word endure means: **"to remain firm under suffering or misfortune without yielding"**. But the Bible offers a much deeper description of the word endure: to be patient, long-suffering and steadfast while looking unto Jesus Who is the author and finisher of our faith (Hebrews 12:2). God's Word, which is the only inspired, infallible and authoritative Holy Scripture teaches that Christians are called to endure trials and tribulations in this Fallen World. Remember, we are pilgrims here in this Fallen World, heading to our final destination, heaven. So in the mean time, we are called to endure. **In fact God wants us not just to endure the way unbelievers do; rather, He wants us to endure with joy!**

WHY ENDURE WITH JOY?

As Christians, the Triune God indwells us by faith (God the Father; God the Son; God the Holy Spirit). So when we choose to call upon God to help us through our hardships (Psalm 46:1-2), and we steadfastly stand on His promises as outlined in the Bible, we will start experiencing the joy of the Lord (Nehemiah 8:10). It is the Lord's joy, not ours. It is a supernatural joy that will provide the supernatural fortitude and grace necessary for us to endure in any difficult circumstance. Keep in mind that even unbelievers can endure hardships and crises; but the difference is that, as Christians, it will be the Lord Jesus Himself working in and through us to overcome the hardships. Thus, we can endure with joy! Here is how I often say it:

Joy is a person—Jesus Christ! Peace is a person —Jesus Christ! And Hope is a person— Jesus Christ! So as you focus on the Lord, you will supernaturally experience His joy, hope, and peace!.

THE JOY OF THE LORD PROVIDES SUPERNATURAL STRENGTH, HOPE, AND PEACE

Personally, I describe the Joy of the Lord as **"a state of walking in deep fellowship with the Triune God, believing that God's absolute Will in every circumstance will be the best!"**. In my experience, joy, peace, and hope are inseparable—as you focus on the source of joy, Jesus Christ, you will experience His perfect peace that surpasses all human reasoning (Isaiah 26:3; John 15:11), and His hope will anchor your soul (Hebrews 6:18-19).

As you turn to the Lord Jesus and His solutions to your hardships, you will be able to focus less on your immediate circumstances and hardships; this will enable you to obtain a Godly perspective about your crisis. Doing this in and of itself will enable the joy, hope, and peace of the Lord to saturate your entire being: Mind, Body and Spirit, and you will be able to endure challenging times in this life with joy. This is a promise, and God is faithful in keeping His Word (Jeremiah 1:12). As the joy of the Lord and His peace saturates your soul (your mind, will, emotions and thinking processes), the physical symptoms of fatigue, weariness, insomnia, fear, anxiety, etc., associated with your hardship, will begin to subside, and then it will become easier for you to endure with joy. No wonder God has called us to endure in this Fallen World with joy. Without the joy of the Lord enabling us, we would be at risk to get into despair, which is not God's will for us.

THE BIBLE ADMONISHES US TO ENDURE WITH JOY

The teaching on enduring trials and tribulations is not

a very popular one, partly because some Christians have been deceived that, once they confess faith in Christ, all of their problems will automatically disappear! But this is Not true! **In fact, once a person genuinely becomes a Christian, he or she becomes a target for the enemy, Satan, the accuser of the brethren, whose primary goal is to kill, steal and destroy** (John 10:10; Revelation 12:10). Notwithstanding, since we live in a Fallen World, the Lord Jesus explicitly warned that we will encounter hardships and various trials in our journey here as pilgrims, but He added that we should be encouraged because He has overcome the world (John 16:33).

The Bible teaches that the Lord Jesus was tempted in every area in life but He never sinned (Hebrews 4:15; 1 Peter 2:22). Thus, He knows exactly what we are going through when we experience various trials and hardships, which is why He is our only hope and solution. And keep in mind that there is **"nothing new under the sun"** (Ecclesiastes 1:9). This means, whatever calamities, hardships, and sufferings you might be experiencing right now is not new to the Human Race, as millions of others in the past have experienced similar hardships and/or the exact same crisis, and God in His faithfulness had enabled them to endure with joy and to overcome.

YOUR PROBLEM IS NOT UNIQUE

Do not allow Satan to deceive you that your circumstance is unique. Here is why: **If Satan succeeds in deceiving you that "no one knows your problem", then it can lead to two potential problems. Firstly, it can cause you to isolate yourself because of shame, thereby preventing you from seeking Godly counsel.** And secondly, it will lead to an erroneously exaggerated perspective of your problem, making it seemingly impossible to endure, which can lead to despair, worsening of the crisis, and various ungodly ways to cope. The solution is simple: Accept God's Word as Truth: there is **"nothing new under the sun"**. God is faithful! — in the same way he had helped millions of others in the past to endure with joy, He is available to help you too! Your job is to depend on His consistent faithfulness!

Several Scriptures teach that your calamity is not unique to you. Below are just a few, so be encouraged!

1 Corinthians 10:13 teaches that:

No temptation has overtaken you except what is common to mankind. And God is faithful; he will not let you be tempted beyond what you can bear. But when you are tempted, he will also provide a way out so that you can endure it (emphasis author's).

Romans 15:4 teaches that:

For everything that was written in the past was written to teach us, so that through the endurance taught in the Scriptures and the encouragement they provide we might have hope (emphasis author's).

As you can see from Romans 15:4, we can be encouraged by the several examples of Godly Men and Women such as Ruth (See the book of Ruth); Esther (See the book of Esther; Job (See the Book of Job), who endured with joy and overcame.

1 Thessalonians 5:16-18 teaches that:

We should,

Rejoice always, pray continually, give thanks in all circumstances; for this is God's will for you in Christ Jesus (emphasis author's)

While this admonition from God may seem impossible during dire pain and suffering, remember that as you depend on God to enable you to endure, all things are possible (Matthew 19:23-26). Additionally, no matter how intense we might perceive our pain and suffering to be, the Bible encourages us to embrace this Godly and eternal perspective: ***"So we fix our eyes not on what is seen, but on what is unseen, since what is seen is temporary, but what is unseen is eternal"*** (2 Corinthians 4:18). According to this encouraging Scripture, whatever your calamities, pains and sufferings are right now, they shall come to pass! — They came to pass! — They are only temporary! Be encouraged and endure with the joy of the Lord.

As you can glean from the above Scriptures, it is God's will that we, as His children, endure with joy and trust Him. Some of you may be saying, **"it's too hard, I can't do it"** because the pain and suffering is unbearable. If this is your experience, right now, and you believe it is beyond your ability to cope, then stand on God's promise in **1 Corinthians 10:13**, and believe that He is with you, always. Here is how God Himself puts it in Deuteronomy 31:8:

> *And the LORD, He is the One who goes before you. He will be with you, He will not leave you nor forsake you; do not fear nor be dismayed.*

How encouraging! Friend, know that God, in His nature is good, and He is fighting for you! He wants you to overcome this trial! You are coming out of this, in Jesus name! So take heart! Proceed now to the next chapter and learn how God has already equipped you to endure with joy and overcome through Christ.

IN CONCLUSION

ℂ Joy is a person —Jesus Christ! Hope is a Person —Jesus Christ! And Peace is a person —Jesus Christ!

ℂ Christians are called to Endure various trials with the joy of the Lord which provides the supernatural ability necessary to endure and overcome;

ℂ We should not get into despair; rather we should stand on God's promises and trust His faithfulness as we endure the various crises we are encountering.

ADDITIONAL RESOURCES

Available @:www.DrRuthTanyi.org/bookstore

1. Faith to Receive God's Promises: How to "Walk" in Biblical Faith and Allow the blessings of God to Chase You;

2. ***Also available in Audio CD/USB Formats:** Faith to Receive God's Promises: How to "Walk" in Biblical Faith and Allow the blessings of God to Chase You.

....

CHAPTER 3

CHRISTIANS ARE EQUIPPED TO ENDURE WITH JOY

But the fruit of the Spirit is love, joy, peace, forbearance, kindness, goodness, faithfulness, gentleness and self-control. Against such things there is no law (Galatians 5:22-23; New International Version, NIV)

As Christians, we serve and worship The God of the Bible Who is fair and just! God will not admonish us to take some kind of action without providing us with the necessary "tools" to do so. Since the Bible teaches that we should endure hardships and calamities in this Fallen World with joy, it implies that God has already equipped us to do so. You may wonder, how? **This is a fair question, and the obvious answer is: Through the Triune God Who indwells each believer; God's Revealed Word; and the presence of the Holy Spirit in and around us.** Let me briefly talk about each of these ways that we are equipped, although these are inseparable in reality.

WE ARE EQUIPPED WITH THE ETERNAL WORD OF GOD

The true Christian Bible, which is the only inspired, infallible and authoritative Word of God has all of the answers to every single problem we will ever experience in this Fallen World. If you are one of those Christians who is still doubting the authenticity of God's Word, then you will struggle to endure with joy and overcome. Most importantly, if your heart is open, begin by asking the Holy Spirit to reveal to you personally, the absolute truth that God's Word as encased in the Bible is trustworthy. Additionally, today in the 21 Century, there are many excellent resources that can help you in your quest to ascertain the trustworthiness of the Bible compared with other pseudo Religious books. I have a book that I believe can help. It is titled: **Can I Trust the Bible as God's Word? What is The Evidence?**

How Do I know? In this book, I discuss the evidence supporting why the true Christian Bible can be trusted. I recommend you obtain a copy.

As I said in the previous chapters, there is no new problem that will befall Mankind that God did not anticipate, and He had already given us the solution in His Word. The problem is that many people do not take the time to invest in knowing God's Word. Yet the Bible teaches that we cannot seperate God from His Word. **Attempting to seek God without His Word is futile, because the Bible teaches that God is His Word — and His Word is Him (i.e., the Living Word, Jesus Christ)** — *"In the beginning was the Word, and the Word was with God, and the Word was God. He was in the beginning with God"* (John 1:1-2, emphasis author's). Thus, knowing God's response and solutions to your hardships require that you know His directives as outlined in His Word.

No matter how severe your pain, suffering, hardship or calamity is, God has equipped you to endure it by revealing His solution to you in His Word. In fact God has elevated His Word above His name (Psalm 138:2). God's Word is perfect and trustworthy (Proverbs 30:5; Psalm 18:30), authenticated by the death, burial, and resurrection of Jesus Christ. There is no advice and/or counsel anyone can give you that will supersede the wisdom found in the Holy Scriptures (Proverbs 21:30). In spite of the blessing of having God's Word readily available to us, compared to the Christians in earlier Centuries who were martyred for possessing the Holy Scriptures, it is rather unfortunate that when calamity "first strikes", some Christians will quickly seek counsel elsewhere before seeking God's response from the Bible. Yet, the solutions available to us in God's Word are always the best.

GOD'S SOLUTIONS ARE ALWAYS THE BEST

God's solution(s) to your crisis may not be as quick as you would like them to be, but they are always the best ones! Take note that often times, it is not God who is delaying the resolution to our crisis. Often times, it is because we are struggling to discern His perfect direction in regards to our calamity. Or at times, people wander off and seek help from other sources first, then turn to God only when things seem impossible. Yet, these other sources cannot provide any permanent solutions to our crisis, because there is only One Truth: Jesus Christ (John 14: 6), Who was and is the Living Word of God. **Rushing to God for help as a last resort is better than not calling upon Him at all; but it requires you to be patient as He "works things out". God is not an ATM Machine which you can just rush to as a last resort and receive an instant resolution to your crisis —No, it does not work like that —you will have to be patient with God as well.**

The Word of God is the only absolute Truth that exists today, and will exist throughout eternity. God's Word is eternal; and is already settled in heaven (Luke 21:33; Psalm 119:89). The Word of God is "alive" and can guide you perfectly through your crisis (Hebrews 4:12). As you stand on God's Word while enduring your calamities, it will sanctify and purify your thinking processes, aligning your thoughts with Godly truths, thus enabling you to endure with joy (John 17:17). Throughout the history of the world, God's Word has provided the necessary comfort which has enabled millions of people to endure hardships; it continues to do so today.

No wonder God's Word as encased in the Bible continues to be the best-selling book of all times.

All so called truths from other sources apart from God's Word are counterfeits and are not sustainable in all things pertaining to life and our existence. Only the truths from God's Word will endure forever (Psalm 119:89).

We are indeed blessed to have God's written Word

available to direct our lives and enable us to endure whatever challenges befall us in this dark world. Believing that God's Word has His solutions is not enough; God wants us to act on His Truths because believing without acting will not yield results in our lives.

GOD REQUIRES US TO ACT ON HIS TRUTHS

Knowing God's solution(s) to your crisis as outlined in His Word requires a response from you: **believing them in your heart and then acting accordingly**—this is true Bible faith, which is what pleases God (Hebrews 11:6). Studying the Word of God and gaining a mental knowing is just the beginning; that knowledge has to get into your heart (the deepest part of your soul) through the process of meditation, and then it will become easier to live it out.

It is only through the art of meditation (a deliberate and constant pondering of God's Word over time), that the Truths in God's Word can begin to saturate your soul, providing the clarity and Godly revelations, which will then enable you to act accordingly.

One way or another, some kind of action from you towards your desired result is required in order for you to receive the manifestation from God. It is a biblical principle that, **"faith without action is useless"** (James 2:14-26). Your action is necessary to complete your faith, making it effective.

At times, the necessary action is readily available in God's Word. For example, God's Word teaches that by the stripes of Jesus we are already healed; this healing took place over 2000 years ago on Calvary's Cross (Isaiah 53:3-5). Therefore, if your current calamity is pain and suffering from a disease, and you believe in your heart in this biblical Truth, then true Bible faith requires that you act on this biblical Truth. This means that by faith, you would have to start acting like someone who is already healed because God's Word says you are, right? Therefore, do not lie in bed all day as a sick person would; instead, to the best of your ability, get out of bed and start acting like you normally would do when you feel healthy, trusting God to strengthen and enable you to endure with joy. As you do this, God, in His faithfulness will honor your faith (Hebrews 11:6).

Do not beg God to heal you; you are already healed by the stripes of Jesus. Your role is to learn to start acting out your faith by practicing how to receive His available healing in your body (Hebrews 5:14). As you endure the process with joy, your physical body will begin to respond and the symptoms of your disease will begin to subside—it works! —I am a living testimony to this biblical truth! For details, obtain my testimonial book: **Healed by the Stripes of Jesus** (See the Additional Resources Section at the end of this chapter).

As another example, God's Word teaches that **"perfect love casts out fear"** (1 John 4:18). Accordingly, do not live in fear of COVID-19; Cancer, Heart Disease or any other calamity you may be encountering right now. Using COVID-19 as another example, act in faith by applying Godly wisdom and discernment and proceed to engage in your daily life, knowing that as you trust God while doing your part (i.e., social distancing, hand washing, etc.), God's love will protect you. If your hardship is financial, especially during this COVID-19 season, do not (hoard, i.e., hide) money; rather, act in faith and genuinely give into God's work as you are able to, and God will be certain to bless you back (Luke 6:38). The worst thing you can do during financial hardship is to act in accordance to your circumstance and stop giving into God's Work; doing so will not be acting in biblical faith (2 Corinthians 5:7).

Acting on God's Word while trusting Him always produces results! The Bible teaches that only the doers receive the blessings from God (James 1:22-25). So do not be deceived: it is not how much you love God; rather, the biblical principle is that God will always honor faith and His Word—God blesses obedience, period! (Hebrews 11: 6; James 1:22-25). Obeying God's Word is not difficult as you might think, but it requires that you completely surrender your will to the leadership of the Holy Spirit who indwells you as a believer. This brings me to the other way God has equipped us to endure with Joy.

WE ARE EQUIPPED WITH THE HOLY SPIRIT

Right before His ascension to Heaven, the Lord Jesus promised to send the Holy Spirit. Here is how He said it, " ... *keep my commands. And I will ask the Father, and he will give you another advocate to help you and be with you forever— the Spirit of truth....*(John 14:15-17). Then, on the day of Pentecost as recorded in Acts chapter 2, the Holy Spirit came. And today, every true follower of Jesus Christ is indwelt and sealed by the Holy Spirit (Ephesians 1:13).

The Holy Spirit, which is the Spirit of Truth, has multiple roles in the life of the believer. But the primary ones are to (1) illuminate Scripture (help us to better understand and apply God's Word in our lives practically); (2) lead and guide our decision making processes in every circumstance; (3) comfort us; (4) provide the supernatural ability necessary to witness for Christ, endure hardships in our personal lives and overcome (John 14:15-31; Acts 1:8). So as Christians, we have the supernatural power within us; that same power that raised the Lord Jesus from the dead is available to enable us to endure calamities in this present world and endure with joy (Romans 8:11).

While the supernatural power from the Holy Spirit is readily available, unfortunately, some Christians are not able to appropriate this power to help them endure hardships because of sin. Sin and disobedience will definitely quench the power and work of the Holy Spirit in your life (Ephesians 4:30; 1 Thessalonians 5:19-22). To resolve this problem and start relying on the Holy Spirit's power to enable you to endure with joy, simply repent from your sinful and disobedient ways.

> *The Christian life is not just difficult to live out in this Fallen World, it is impossible to do without the empowerment from the Holy Spirit, much worse to endure hardships.*

As a child of God, you have been blessed with that same power that raised the Lord Jesus from the dead — rely on it — depend on it — trust and then obey it! Most importantly, remember to invite the Holy Spirit to help you, always; make Him your friend, because He is! The Holy Spirit is a "gentleman" and He will not intrude in your life without your permission. So we have to continually seek His direction and leadership, and surrender daily to His wisdom (Matthew 7:7).

You are an overcomer in Christ, and the Spirit of God in you is far more superior than any other spirits out there in the world (1 John 4:4). But God requires that you allow His Spirit to help you to endure with joy and overcome. Here is how the Bible puts it, *"Now all glory to God, who is able, through his mighty power at work within us, to accomplish infinitely more than we might ask or think* (Ephesians 3:20, NLT). God is willing to do way more than most of us can even imagine or ask Him, so trust Him. While it may sound impossible to endure certain hardships, God has also equipped each believer with His Fruit, the Fruit of the Spirit, to enable us to accomplish those seemingly impossible calamities.

WE ARE EQUIPPED WITH THE FRUIT OF THE SPIRIT

There are times when it may seem useless to even ask God for strength to endure hardships, pains, and sufferings. I understand exactly how this feels; I experienced weariness in the journey fighting cancer as well. But the absolute truth is that, as Christians, we are well equipped to endure the worst circumstances life has to offer. This is primarily because our Lord and Savior Jesus Christ completely understands our personal sufferings since He Himself experienced every kind of hardship and even worse (the crucifixion); so He is compassionate, and He will never leave or forsake us (Deuteronomy 31:6). Secondarily, as Christians, we have the qualities of the Triune God in us, the Fruit of the Spirit, to enable us to endure any circumstance we will ever encounter in this life. Galatians 5:22-23 describes it this way: ***But the fruit of the Spirit is love, joy, peace, forbearance, kindness, goodness, faithfulness, gentleness and self-control. Against such things there is no law.***

Take note that the qualities/attributes of the Triune God as described in Galatians 5:22-23 are already indwelling you, the child of God. Also, know that the "Fruit" of the Spirit, is in the singular in the Godhead, and not in the plural, although 9 qualities/attributes are described. And as you can readily see in Galatians 5:22-23, God has equipped you with the quality of **"forbearance"** (i.e., patience), which is necessary to endure hardships with joy. Just like everything else with God, it is your responsibility to believe that God's Spirit which indwells you is readily available to empower you, and then by faith, you would have to act in accordance with His directives in His Word. Also, take note that **"Joy"** is another quality of God's Spirit indwelling you. Therefore, make a decision to focus on the Prince of Joy — Jesus Christ, and allow His Joy to enable you to endure.

Friend, you can endure with joy and overcome! Do not give up! God is on your side! He has already preordained and equipped you to win the battles in this dark world. **Your job is to approach Him with childlike faith, surrender your calamities to Him, and then trust His perfect wisdom. He is for you and Not against you! God is a good, good Father, Who has blessed us with everything we need to partake in His Kingdom** (See Ephesians chapters 1 & 2; 2 Peter 1: 2-4). Do you believe these things? Since God has already equipped us to endure with joy, the next logical question is: **How do we endure?** Proceed now to the next chapter to learn how.

IN CONCLUSION

ಐ God has equipped Christians with His Revealed Word; the Holy Spirit; and the Fruit of the Spirit, so we can endure the various hardships and calamities in this dark world;

ಐ Living in sin and disobedience will quench the power and work of the Holy Spirit in our lives;

ಐ In order for us to receive God's promises, our faith in God's Word must accompany some kind of corresponding action.

ADDITIONAL RESOURCES

Available @:www.DrRuthTanyi.org/bookstore

1. Healed By the Stripes of Jesus! My Story! My Miracle! How I overcame Metastasis Colon Cancer! You can Be Healed Too!

2. ***Abridged Version Available in Audio CD/USB Formats:** Healed By the Stripes of Jesus! My Story! My Miracle! How I overcame Metastasis Colon Cancer! You can Be Healed Too!

3. Faith to Receive God's Promises: How to "Walk" in Biblical Faith and Allow the blessings of God to Chase You;

4. **Available in Audio CD/USB Formats:** Faith to Receive God's Promises: How to "Walk" in Biblical Faith and Allow the blessings of God to Chase You.

....

CHAPTER 4

HOW DO WE ENDURE WITH JOY?

Therefore,... let us run with perseverance the race marked out for us, fixing our eyes on Jesus, the pioneer and perfecter of faith. For the joy set before him he endured the Cross, scorning its shame, and sat down at the right hand of the throne of God (Hebrews 12:1-2, New International Version, NIV)

Hopefully you are in agreement that God has called and equipped us to endure hardships with joy. Since that is the case, you may be asking yourself: **How do I go about this? How do I endure with joy when there is nothing to be joyful about?** This is a very fair question because at times our problems may appear insurmountable, but with God, nothing is impossible (Matthew 19:26). The Bible teaches that there is a way that seem right to a person, but the end is destruction (Proverbs 14:12).

While there are many potential solutions to your crisis, choosing God's ways to endure and overcome during crisis is the best decision you will ever make, and it will require that you maintain a Godly perspective by learning how to (1) become God conscious; (2) overcome "emotional bumps" in your paths; (3) stop following the crowd; (4) act on Godly Truths with a childlike faith; and (5) depend on God's love and His consistent character.

Just like a marathon runner trains him or herself to endure the race, we too, as Christians, have to train ourselves to maintain a Godly perspective and be eternally focused during crisis, in order to endure with joy. As the above Scripture is teaching, the Lord Jesus was eternally focused, which enabled Him to endure the Cross with joy — we can do likewise. Maintaining a Godly perspective is the key to your ability to endure with joy (Hebrews

5:12-20, 12:1-2). I proceed now to discuss some recommendations for maintaining a Godly perspective while enduring with joy.

MAINTAINING A GODLY PERSPECTIVE

We are in a marathon, and Godly wisdom is necessary to endure the race here on earth. Endurance is a measure of one's ability to sustain during hardships, and it is a process that can potentially lead to weariness, fatigue, and feelings of discouragement. Therefore, becoming God conscious is necessary to enable you to endure with joy.

BECOME GOD CONSCIOUS

It is God's will that we, His children live in a manner in which we are consciously aware of His presence and working in our lives. By doing so, it will inadvertently enable us to become 100% dependent on Him. Becoming God conscious may appear simple, but it requires that you make a deliberate effort to surrender your will, plans, thoughts, etc., to God. This can be difficult to do in this 21st Century as we are living in the so called "Information Age", with all kinds of ungodly information and advice readily available to us. But as I discussed earlier, we have God's complete counsel available to us in His Revealed Word, and no plan in life can succeed beyond the Lord's (Proverbs 21:30).

To become God conscious requires that you spend extra time studying and meditating on Godly truths. Meditation will require some effort from you! But it will be well worth it! As you take the extra time to ponder, think, and reflect on Godly Truths (i.e., meditating), the Holy Spirit will begin to strengthen you, and reveal Godly wisdom and ways for you to endure and overcome. As you become 100% dependent on God by spending time meditating on His Truths, you will become God conscious. This will then allow the Holy Spirit to do His job to embolden you with the supernatural ability required for you to endure with joy. As you become emboldened, you will in turn be able to overcome calamities with minimal effort, because it will be God Himself working in and through you.

The Lord Jesus even taught this principle of becoming God conscious/dependent in Matthew 6:33. He said: ***"But seek first his kingdom and his righteousness, and all these things will be given to you as well"***. Although in context the Lord was teaching about physical things such as clothing, food, etc., this principle is very applicable in every other area in our lives. Becoming God conscious was one of the major principles I practiced throughout my fight with cancer, and even today.

During the initial year fighting Metastasis Colon cancer, I spent several hours daily studying and meditating on Godly Truths such as the fact that I was already healed by the stripes of Jesus. As I was meditating on Godly Truths about healing, I became extremely God conscious and my focus switched 100% away from the Cancer diagnosis, which enabled me to overcome fear, anxiety, etc. Then, a few months thereafter, I received the revelation from the Holy Spirit that I was completely healed from the Cancer. Although it took several years for the physical manifestation of my healing to be evident, that revelation from the Holy Spirit provided the supernatural ability that enabled me to endure with joy, even before I saw the manifestation.

Friend, surrender your crisis to God right now, become 100% God conscious and dependent, and trust Him with the outcome — it will be a good outcome!

As you are depending on God, it is necessary to learn how to overcome various "emotional hurdles" you may encounter in your journey.

OVERCOME YOUR "EMOTIONAL HURDLES"

Usually, as part of the human experience, the feelings and/or emotions of fear, anxiety, uncertainties, doubt, etc., are often present during the process of enduring whatever crisis we might be experiencing. I call these "emotional hurdles," because they have the potential to impede your progress if you do not learn how to overcome them. Although Christians are indwelt with the Triune God, we are still human beings, and as such, we are not absolved from experiencing these frightening and often discouraging feelings and/or emotions. Experiencing these emotions in and of themselves does not mean that we have sinned, are weak in faith, or are not abiding in Christ. Rather, how we handle these "emotional hurdles" is what determines how fast we overcome our crisis.

According to the Diagnostic and Statistical Manual of Mental Disorders (DSM-5), the powerful and often paralyzing emotion of fear can be described as chronic anticipation of an impending doom/negative outcome. The best and only effective way to overcome the fear associated with your current crisis is to meditate on the love of God. The Bible teaches that the only antidote to fear is having a deeper revelation of how much God loves you (1 John 4:18).

According to God's Word, if you are chronically living in fear and unable to overcome the fearful emotion, it means that you do not yet have a deeper revelation of God's love to you. This Truth is not intended to cause you to experience shame and guilt, which is not your portion in Christ (Romans 8:1-2); instead, it is intended to help you to realize that you need to spend more time meditating on how much God loves you. God loves you enough that He demonstrated His love for you on the Cross over 2000 years ago while you were still a sinner (Romans 5:8). Think about that!—He loves you much more now, as a Christian!

The Bible teaches about a Godly fear, which is wisdom (Proverbs 9:10). But the emotion of fear, which comes from the anticipation of a negative outcome, is a demonic spirit. This kind of pathological fear leads to emotional death. Here is how the Bible describes it, **"There is no fear in love. But perfect love drives out fear, because fear has to do with punishment. The**

one who fears is not made perfect in love" (1 John 4:18).

FEAR— FALSE EVIDENCE APPEARING REAL

The emotion of fear to a Christian is just like a shadow, it is not real! I describe fear as — **False Evidence Appearing Real!** Because your reality is found in Christ, who will never leave or forsake you; He is always with you, and nothing will ever separate you from His perfect love (Hebrews 13:5; Romans 8:38-39). Hence, in the name of Jesus, and the power of the Holy Spirit, confront your fears today. Do not allow the fearful emotion to hinder your progress, because it will, if you do not address it.

Feelings of anxiety and uncertainties are other "emotional hurdles" you must overcome. The underlying cause of anxiety is fear! Dealing with the anxieties and uncertainties about the potential outcome of your crisis can be debilitating. It can be debilitating because with your finite mind and reasoning abilities you cannot perfectly project the outcome; so it is best to learn how to trust God instead.

Just like fear, DSM-5 describes generalized anxiety as a chronic anticipation of a negative outcome. As a Christian, God knows the number of hairs on your head; He knows you intimately, and He has promised that He knows your needs even before you pray (Luke 12:7). With such a promise from a faithful God, He wants you to stop leaning on your own understanding and instead, start trusting His promises (Proverbs 3:5-6). Being anxious about your current calamity implies that you do not trust God, and as such, you are unable to depend on Him for help. **The bottom line is this: Anxiety is a "crisis in faith" — You are either doubting God's promises or you are meditating on your problems instead of walking by faith** (2 Corinthians 5:7).

REFOCUSING ON JESUS

As easy as this might sound, the "emotional hurdles" of anxiety, doubt, and fear can easily be overcome by redirecting your focus back to the Lord Jesus, as the Apostle Peter did when he started to sink into the Sea in his attempt to walk on water. The Bible tells the story how the Apostle Peter, by faith, intently focused on Jesus, started to walk on water, something that only Jesus has ever done in the history of the world. But when the Apostle Peter took his eyes off of Jesus and started looking at the frightening waves and the turbulence of the sea, he immediately experienced fear, anxiety, doubt, and as such, he started to sink into the water. But as he refocused and fixed his gaze onto Jesus and called out for His help, the Lord rescued him from drowning. Likewise, when you take your attention off of Jesus and start looking into your circumstances, it will lead to fear, anxiety, doubt and despair. So, just like the Apostle Peter taught us, if you are experiencing these emotions, refocus, start meditating on God's Word, and fix your gaze onto Jesus.

The Bible teaches that as we focus on the Lord Jesus as our refuge and strength, we will in turn experience His peace (Isaiah 26:3), and the emotions of anxiety, fear, and doubt will start to subside.

Brethren, the only True cure to these "emotional hurdles" is focusing on the Lord Jesus. Anti anxiety drugs do not work, and will never work! There are no medications to overcoming fears and doubt. Only the Truths in God's Word provide the antidote.

A LESSON ON OVERCOMING DOUBT

While in prison, John the Baptist started doubting if the Lord Jesus was indeed the Messiah; thus in his attempt to seek the truth, he sent his disciples to question Jesus. And guess what the Lord's response was? He told John's disciples to tell John to go and study the Scriptures again. Why was this? Because the Old Testament had prophesied the kinds of miracles the Messiah would perform, thereby validating His identity. Accordingly, Jesus pointed John the Baptist back to God's Word, the only source of Truth, in order for him to study the evidence and overcome his doubt. This is a powerful lesson on how to overcome doubt. **Friend, if you are doubting that God is with you through your calamity, just like Jesus told John, I am telling you the same thing: Go to God's Word, meditate and stand on His promises.** God's Word is the only cure to overcoming your doubts. As you are doing your best to overcome these "emotional hurdles" in your path while you endure, be steadfast in upholding God's opinion and do not allow the opinions of others to distract you.

AVOID DEPENDING ON THE OPINIONS OF OTHERS

To endure your crisis with joy will require that you elevate God's opinion above every other opinion out there. Remember, to be God dependent means that you strive to reach "a place" in your life where you make a decision that God's ways are the best! This is hard for many people to accept, because as I said earlier, there are many other potential solutions to your crisis "out there". But these potential solutions will not foster a permanent and/or a peaceful resolution as God's Word will do. So, if you make the mistake to "go with the crowd", meaning to resolve your crisis like "everybody else" is doing by using various ungodly methods, then you will "crash". The Lord Jesus teaches that elevating the opinions of others above God's Word will lead to unbelief (John 5:44). Unbelief will eventually quench the power of the Holy Spirit in your life, and you will in turn experience the emotion of despair (Proverbs 14:12; Ephesians 4:30).

It can be tempting to choose the most popular ways of resolving crisis, especially because unfortunately, God's ways are not too popular nowadays. But if you want to endure without despair, be patient with God. Additionally, knowing your identity as a child of God will definitely empower and enable you to endure with joy. Due to limited space in this book, I cannot delve much into this relevant topic of your identity in Christ, so I recommend my book: **Are You Moving Forward with Jesus? How to Excel in Your Identity in Christ.** This biblically-based book will help you, I believe. As you are being emboldened by the Holy Spirit, appropriating your inherited power and authority in the name of Jesus is necessary in order for you to endure with joy.

ACT IN FAITH

To endure with joy requires that you act on Godly truths. I explained earlier how faith without acting in accordance with God's Word is essentially useless (James 2:14-26). The biggest misconception about faith is that people erroneously believe they do not have enough faith to receive God's promises. But this notion is scripturally incorrect, because the Bible teaches that we all have faith in our born again spirits (Galatians 5:22-23; 2 Peter 1:1), but some individuals are not growing in their faith because they do not act on Godly truths. The more you act on Godly truths, the more opportunities you will give the Holy Spirit to strengthen your faith, and you will begin to experience more manifestations of God's promises in your life (Hebrews 11:6). Another misconception about faith is that, faith is ineffective in the presence of fear, doubt, and anxiety.

Again, this is a lie! True Bible faith is acting on God's Word regardless of your emotions, and then trusting Him with the results.

The Bible has numerous examples of individuals who endured with joy as they acted contrary to their fearful, anxious, and/or doubtful emotions, and God accomplished much through them (e.g., See the Books of Joshua; Esther; Ruth; etc). Hence, to start the process of strengthening your faith, find a promise in God's Word in regards to your problem and start acting on it accordingly. There is always a solution in God's Word either stated explicitly or through a principle taught in the Bible. If you are unable to find the solution, seek Godly counsel from a Bible believing and practicing Minister; Pastor, etc., or even a seasoned Christian, then meditate and pray, and allow the Holy Spirit to confirm it in your spirit. Once you have clarity from the Holy Spirit, accordingly, act on the solution and trust God.

REST IN GOD'S LOVE

Remember that as a child of God, you are securely protected in God's perfect love for you (Romans 8:38-39). Having a revelation of God's love for you will enable you to endure and overcome crises and/or calamities you will experience in this life. If nothing else seems to be working for you right now, I recommended that you set aside extra time and start meditating on how much God loves you. **Love never fails!** When you die and meet the Lord face to face, your faith and hope in Him will be completed; nevertheless, your love for Him and His love for you will endure forevermore! God's love for you is constant — it will never change!(1 Corinthians 13:1-13).

As you start to gain a deeper revelation of God's love for you (i.e., Agape love, meaning unconditional love), that Truth will serve as an antidote against the worries/anxieties about your current crisis. You know why? Because God's kind of love towards you means He is protecting and preserving you throughout your calamity (1 Corinthians 13: 4-12). Friend, God is not angry at you! — He is pleased with your efforts as you are enduring with joy! He desires for you to overcome whatever your crisis is right now. Do you believe this?

TRUST GOD'S CONSISTENT NATURE/CHARACTER

In my experience in ministry, many Christians love God, but they do not take the time to meditate on His Holy and consistent nature. **For instance, the Bible teaches that God can never lie — He is faithful, loving, compassionate, consistent, gracious, merciful, forgiving, just, etc., etc. If you were to meditate on each of these qualities of God, you will quickly realize that God is for you, not against you.** With this knowledge, it should be settled in your heart that God is not pleased that you are undergoing this crisis —He wants you to overcome this calamity.

Friend, having this understanding about the nature of God is a faith builder, which will foster hope and joy as you endure.

Again, if all else fail, meditate and "rest" on God's faithful and consistent nature (Numbers 23:19; Titus 1:2; Exodus 34:6-8; John 3:16; 1 John 4:7-8; Hebrews 13:8). And remember, in the same way God had helped millions of others in the past with similar or the exact type of crisis; likewise, He is helping you right now — so be encouraged! If you need additional teaching material about the nature of God, I have an audio CD teaching that will help you. It is titled: **The True Christian Bible: From God To You!** Refer to the "Additional Resources" section at the end of this chapter and find out how to obtain a copy.

REMEMBER TO ALWAYS PRAY AND WORSHIP GOD

Throughout this book, I have talked about meditating on God's Word, which is a form of prayer. Additionally, remember to stay prayerful, regardless of your circumstance (1 Thessalonians 5:16-18). Do not wait to feel like praying before you pray. Rather, just pray, which is simply communication with God. Even when you are too tired and/or you do not know how to pray, ask the Holy Spirit to enable you to pray, and He will do so (Romans 8:26-27).

Another powerful way to endure crisis and overcome is through praising and worshiping God. Praise and worship will shift your focus away from you, onto God, and it is an excellent antidote against fear and anxiety (Acts 16:25-26). This is because the emotions of praising and worshipping God and the ungodly emotions of fear and anxiety are mutually exclusive; meaning, both cannot dominate in your soul at the same time. Hence, genuinely praising and worshipping God will cause the ungodly emotions of fear and anxiety to supernaturally dissipate. So create some extra time to continuously praise and worship God, Who deserves your worship and adoration! As you are putting into practice the above recommendations, know that there are Godly rewards awaiting you! You will not regret the time spent in seeking God. Proceed now to the next chapter to learn more on the benefits of enduring with joy.

IN CONCLUSION

- ෂ True Bible faith requires that we act on Godly Truths regardless of how we feel;

- ෂ Knowing our identity in Christ will enable us to endure crises with joy and overcome;

- ෂ Enduring with joy requires that we become God Conscious; overcome various "emotional hurdles"; choose God's opinions above others; and act in faith

ADDITIONAL RESOURCES

Available @:www.DrRuthTanyi.org/bookstore

1. Faith to Receive God's Promises: How to "Walk" in Biblical Faith and Allow the blessings of God to Chase You;

2. ***Also available in Audio CD/USB Formats:** Faith to Receive God's Promises: How to "Walk" in Biblical Faith and Allow the blessings of God to Chase You;

3. Are you Moving Forward with Jesus? How to Excel in Your Identity in Christ;

4. ***Also available in Audio CD/USB Formats:** Are you Moving Forward with Jesus? How to Excel in Your Identity in Christ;

5. Can I trust the Bible as God's Word? How Do I Know? What Is The Evidence?

6. *** Available in Audio CD/USB Formats:** The True Christian Bible: From God To You!: Do Not Be Deceived! Know The Truth!

....

CHAPTER 5

ENDURANCE YIELDS GODLY REWARDS

Jesus also said, "The Kingdom of God is like a farmer who scatters seed on the ground. Night and day, while he's asleep or awake, the seed sprouts and grows, but he does not understand how it happens. The earth produces the crops on its own. First a leaf blade pushes through, then the heads of wheat are formed, and finally the grain ripens (Mark 4:26-28, New International Version, NIV)

When God admonishes us to believe and act in accordance with His Word, it is because of the countless benefits that we will enjoy in this life and in all eternity. As the Scripture above teaches, the Kingdom of God works through a process of Seed, Time, and Harvest. **The Seed is the Word of God that we meditate on, and then we have to "walk" and act by faith and trust God through the process of time; then the harvest or manifestation of those promises will be evident in our lives in God's perfect timing.**

Several Scriptures teach that enduring hardships with joy has countless manifestations of rewards. While God does not use crisis, calamities and hardships to punish us, He will use them to strengthen our faith, if we allow Him to (Isaiah 40:31). The Bible teaches that God can use even the worst circumstances to conform us into the image of Christ, if we are willing to allow Him to do so (Romans 8:28-29).

While you may question whether or not some kind of benefit will result from your crisis, I guarantee you, based on the authority of God's Word— it will, if you totally surrender to the process and trust God's wisdom. Your job is not to figure out how and when, but to trust God with the outcome. It is almost 12 years since I was diagnosed with Metastatic Colon Cancer, and if someone would have told me that my testimony will be helping countless of people, I would not have believed it. But today, because I allowed the Holy Spirit to enable me to endure with joy, I was able to overcome, and God is using my experience to strengthen and encourage countless of individuals.

Just knowing that enduring with joy produces countless benefits is a faith builder during crisis. The Bible teaches that as the Lord Jesus focused on the outcome of His crucifixion (i.e., the joy to see Mankind saved), He was able to endure Calvary's Cross (Hebrews 12:1-2). Likewise, choose to focus on the blessed benefits God has promised those who endure with joy. Interestingly, calamities have a way of drawing people closer to God, which will be an excellent thing. **For some of you, this current crisis you are experiencing is teaching you that you needed to depend more on God, which I believe is good for you long-term, right? For others, your current hardship is enabling you to approach life from a Godly perspective, again another great thing, right? These are already excellent benefits as you can perceive.**

The Biblical principle is that, if we allow God to work in and through us as we endure hardships in life, we will always come out victorious. Keep in mind that as a Christian, you are already victorious in Christ. Therefore, as an example, if your crisis is a terminal disease, and you die prematurely without receiving your physical healing in this life, it will still be a victory because you will be ushered into the presence of the Lord where there is no pain, sorrow, and suffering (Philippians 1:21). And if you overcome the disease in this life, it will still be a victory because you will have a blessed testimony to shame the devil, glorify God, and encourage others. So it is always a win-win situation for you, a child of God! — so be encouraged! Below are other promises from God awaiting you, as you endure with joy!

THE BLESSINGS OF ENDURING WITH JOY!

GOD WILL REWARD YOUR EFFORTS ABUNDANTLY

God has promised that as you remain steadfast in His promises while enduring your crisis, you will definitely reap a Godly harvest if you do not quit. You may not understand how your harvest will manifest, but it will. Here is one encouraging promise:

Do not be deceived: God cannot be mocked. A man reaps what he sows. Whoever sows to please their flesh, from the flesh will reap destruction; whoever sows to please the Spirit, from the Spirit will reap eternal life. Let us not become weary in doing good, for at the proper time we will reap a harvest if we do not give up (Galatians 6:7-9; emphasis author's)

YOU WILL EXPERIENCE A DEEPER RELATIONSHIP WITH GOD

God has promised that it is a blessing when we choose to depend on Him as we endure through our trials and tribulations, so take heart! Here is another promise:

Blessed is the one who perseveres under trial because, having stood the test, that person will receive the crown of life that the Lord has promised to those who love him (James 1:12; emphasis author's)

YOUR CHARACTER WILL BEGIN TO BE CHRIST-LIKE

The irony about enduring calamities with joy is that, the process is often the best teacher in and of itself. Because through it all, you will start learning the art of waiting on God's perfect timing (i.e., patience), humbling yourself and relying on His wisdom; these are all Christ-like qualities that are beneficial to your relationship with God and others.

Crises truly provide God with the opportunity to start "molding and shaping" us into the image of Christ, which is His ultimate will for the believer (Romans 8:28-30).

Here is an exemplary promise from God that describes this process:

And we know that in all things God works for the good of those who love him, who have been called according to his purpose. For those God foreknew he also predestined to be conformed to the image of his Son, that he might be the firstborn among many brothers and sisters. And those he predestined, he also called; those he called, he also justified; those he justified, he also glorified (Romans 8:28-30, emphasis author's).

As you can see from the above Scripture, as a child of God, every circumstance in your life is working out to your advantage—hallelujah! Do you believe this? God has promised those of us who love Him that all things will indeed work out for our good! No matter how horrible your current crisis is right now, allow God to use it for His glory and to "mold and shape" your character to be Christ-like.

YOU WILL BECOME MORE HOPEFUL

Another irony about calamities is that they present us with two potential options: To be more hopeful in God's promises or to become hopeless. Hopelessness, which is the primary cause of depression, is not the lot for a child of God.

Having hope in the Triune God should be the anchor of our souls daily, especially during crisis, as it will foster Christ-like qualities in us.

Here is how God states it:

Not only so, but we also glory in our sufferings, because we know that suffering produces perseverance; perseverance, character; and character, hope. And hope does not put us to shame, because God's love has been poured out into our hearts through the Holy Spirit, who has been given to us (Romans 5: 3-5; emphasis authors).

Here is another promise from God for those who depend on Him:

The LORD is good to those whose hope is in him, to the one who seeks him...(Lamentations 3:25; emphasis authors).

Here is another powerful promise from God, encouraging you to be hopeful.

I waited patiently for the LORD; he turned to me and heard my cry. He lifted me out of the slimy pit, out of the mud and mire; he set my feet on a rock and gave me a firm place to stand (Psalm 40:1-2; emphasis authors).

YOU WILL GAIN GODLY WISDOM, PATIENCE, AND SELF-CONTROL

Crisis will teach you to become patient, a Christ-like quality that is very much needed today among Christians and Non-Christians alike. As you are being patient, it will give God the opportunity to do His work in and through you, and you will begin to embrace a Godly perspective which is necessary for you to overcome. Here is a promise from God:

Whoever is patient has great understanding, but one who is quick-tempered displays folly (Proverbs 14:29; emphasis author's)

Being patient will also enable you to master the art of self-control in all circumstances. Here is an encouraging promise from God to you:

Better a patient person than a warrior, one with self-control than one who takes a city. (Proverbs 16:32; emphasis author's).

YOU WILL BECOME BETTER EQUIPPED TO OVERCOME FUTURE CRISIS

In my view, a significant benefit of enduring with joy is that you will be well equipped to overcome future crisis in this life. You will indeed encounter future crisis since we live in a Fallen World. But the difference is that, you will have learnt how to depend on God and His strength. Here is how the Old Testament Prophet Isaiah describes the process: *But those who wait on the LORD Shall renew their strength; They shall mount up with wings like eagles, They shall run and not be weary, They shall walk and not faint* (Isaiah 40:31, NKJV; emphasis author's). So take heart, as the Psalmist said, **"Wait for the LORD; be strong and take heart and wait for the LORD** (Psalms 27:14; emphasis author's). As the Apostle James said under the inspiration of the Holy Spirit, you will inherit the "crown of life"! Brethren, to endure with joy is worth it!

WHY PEOPLE FAIL TO ENDURE WITH JOY

In spite of all of the rewards that await those who choose to endure with joy while depending on the Lord; people fail to endure with joy because they reject God's ways (already discussed throughout this book) in overcoming their calamities. To resolve this issue and prevent getting into despair and depression, simply make a decision to seek God and He will accept your request.

God does not turn anyone away. Jesus explained it this way: *Ask and it will be given to you; seek and you will find; knock and the door will be opened to you. For everyone who asks receives; the one who seeks finds; and to the one who knocks, the door will be opened* (Matthew 7:7-8; emphasis author's). Do not be deceived, the primary reason people get into despair and depression from crisis is because they attempt to resolve their problems while relying on their own wisdom and abilities.

> *Friend, avoid depression, become hopeful as you seek God's help. There are no "quick fixes" to the majority of life's calamities, so be patient and trust God!*

I hope you have been encouraged to continue your journey of enduring with joy. Also, I highly recommend that you go back and reread this entire book, start meditating on the Scriptures discussed herein. Now, proceed to the next page for some concluding remarks.

IN CONCLUSION

„ It is always for our benefit when God admonishes us to believe and act on His Word;

„ Enduring during crisis has countless benefits in this life and in eternity;

„ People fail to endure during crisis and end up in despair and depression because they reject God's Ways of overcoming their calamities.

ADDITIONAL RESOURCES

Available @:www.DrRuthTanyi.org/bookstore

*All Available in Audio CD/USB Formats

1. Holy-Spirit-Led Healthy Emotions: The Fruit of The Spirit and Your Health;

2. Did God Really Say That? How to Overcome Doubt and Receive God's Promises: Life-Changing Lessons Learned From Overcoming Metastasis Colon Cancer;

3. Live Above your Fears and Overcome Sicknesses and Diseases;

4. Be Anxious No more!

CONCLUDING REMARKS

The godly may trip seven times, but they will get up again. But one disaster is enough to overthrow the wicked. (Proverbs 24:16, New Living Translation; NLT).

I am trusting God that He has used the teaching in this book to strengthen you, and you are enduring whatever crisis you are currently experiencing with joy. As I mentioned, "this too shall come to pass"! Trials, tribulations, pains, sufferings, are all part of the human experience. As already discussed, even very Godly individuals will experience their share of hardships in this Fallen World; experiencing hardships simply means that you are a human being!

Since every human being will experience some kind of hardship in this lifetime, how we allow God to enable us to overcome our calamities is what really matters. **As I have already discussed, it is up to you, and not God, how you triumph during your crisis. Remember that as a Christian, God has already equipped you to overcome the calamity you are experiencing right now!** You are not alone in this "battle"! God is with you! Hence, approach this season in your life as an opportunity to learn all of the lessons you can— it will be beneficial to you over time.

As I have shared throughout this book, if a person would have told me 12 years ago that, someday, God would be using the cancer experience I suffered from to minister to countless of individuals, I would not have considered that perspective. Nonetheless, as I endured, today, my testimony is encouraging countless of individuals.

Friend, do not give up on God! Do not give up on yourself! You can do this! It is coming to pass! In fact, it came to pass! Allow the wisdom, power, and strength from the Triune God and His Revealed Word, to guide you daily.

You are an overcomer through Christ—live daily in His power and authority!

God has promised that, even when we make mistakes, He is available to help us: So stand up in the name of Jesus and keep moving forward. God has told us that: *"The godly may trip seven times, but they will get up again. But one disaster is enough to overthrow the wicked"* (Proverbs 24:16, NLT; emphasis author's).

Also remember this promise from God that He is watching over you: *"The LORD directs the steps of the godly. He delights in every detail of their lives. Though they stumble, they will never fall, for the LORD holds them by the hand"* (Psalm 37:23-24, NLT; emphasis author's). Friend, God loves you—Rise up from your calamity and move forward—You are called to endure with joy! You can do this through Christ Jesus, Amen! (Philippians 4:13).

Concluding Remarks

---------------------------------- † ----------------------------------

ACCEPT JESUS NOW!

Jesus told him, "I am the way, the truth, and the life. No one can come to the Father except through me..." (John 14:6-7; New International Version, NIV).

We live in a Fallen World! Things will only be perfect at the second coming of Jesus Christ, or if as a Christian, you die and meet the Lord before His second return. Believe it or not, you will die someday, and the Lord's second return is imminent (Acts 1:11). Only God knows your heart. Throughout this book, I have talked about the Lord Jesus as the Messiah: Savior of Mankind from that Sinful Nature each of us inherited at the time of our natural birth into this world, because of the transgression by Adam and Eve as recorded in Genesis chapter three.

You may attend Church or other Christian functions regularly, but have you personally asked the Lord Jesus to come into your life? Do you know for sure? If not, I want to give you the opportunity to do so, right now, because you want to be certain where you will spend eternity. The Lord Jesus is the only human being in the history of the world who can guarantee that you will spend eternity in the presence of God.

There is only One True Living God, the God of the True Christian Bible, Creator of the Heavens and the Earth; and having a relationship with this God is only possible through His Son, Jesus Christ (John 14:6).

Jesus Christ was/is 100% God and was/is100% human being, and He backed up His claims with eye witness verifiable evidence: He raised the dead; performed unmatched miracles; He Himself was raised from the dead; etc. Jesus Christ fulfilled all of God's perfect Laws 100%, something that no human being in the history of the world has ever done and will ever do. Jesus

Himself said: **"I am the way, the truth, and the life. No one can come to the Father except through me"** (John 14:6-7; emphasis author's). The Lord Jesus said all other so called Religious Leaders before and after Him are liars and thieves (John 10:8). In fact, these other Religious Leaders are all dead and still in their graves. Only Jesus Christ is alive today, seated at the right hand of God the Father (Acts 7:55-56; Romans 8:34; Ephesians 1:20).

Jesus died so that you can have a blessed, abundant, and fulfilling life here on the earth and in all eternity (John 10:10). He wants to help you to "do life". He loves you unconditionally and died for your sins: **"For this is how God loved the world: He gave his one and only Son, so that everyone who believes in him will not perish but have eternal life"** (John 3:16, NLT). God wants to bless you with a Brand New Nature and deliver you from the hands of the Evil One, Satan; from yourself; and then He wants to spend eternity with you upon your death.

The Bible teaches that if you believe in your heart in the Lord Jesus as the Messiah, and you confess that God the Father raised Him from the dead, you will be saved (i.e., be redeemed from your Sinful Nature) (Romans 10:9).

If you genuinely believe in the Lord Jesus in your heart and are ready to confess Him as your personal Lord and Savior, then simply repeat the prayer below: Know that, believing first in your heart is what really matters to God, and the out loud confession is a way of stating what you already believed. Here is the prayer:

"Dear God, I thank You for sending Jesus to die for my sins. I believe in my heart, and I am now confessing with my mouth that Jesus died for my sins, and on the third day You raised Him from the dead. Today, I ask You, Jesus, to come into my heart and change me. By faith, I believe You have accepted me. From this day forward, I declare I am a follower of Jesus Christ! Thank

You God, in Jesus name, Amen!"

Friend, if you said that prayer genuinely, based on the authority of God's Word, I declare you are a Christian. God now knows you personally (Matthew 10:30)! He has sealed you with His Holy Spirit (Ephesians 1:13), and according to Jesus, no one will ever snatch you from His hands (John 10:28-29)—Hallelujah—Glory to God!

Welcome into the Kingdom of Light, God's kingdom. Please, will you contact us so that we can send you teaching materials to help you grow in your journey and relationship with God? We want to help you!

Contact Information
on Next Page →

CONTACT INFORMATION

---✝---

Dr Ruth Tanyi Ministries, Inc.

P O BOX 1806

Loma Linda; CA; 92354; USA

Website: www.DrRuthTanyi.org

Email: Info@DrRuthTanyi.org

To Donate to Our Ministry, please visit:
www.DrRuthTanyi.org/donate

FOR MORE TEACHINGS BY DR TANYI

---- ✝ ----

- ❧ Subscribe to Our YouTube Channel > Search Dr Ruth Tanyi Ministries Inc on YouTube

- ❧ Follow Us on Facebook > Search Dr Ruth Tanyi Ministries Inc on Facebook

- ❧ Sign up to receive Our Monthly Newsletters > Visit our website and sign up there: www.DrRuthTanyi.org

- ❧ Subscribe to our Bible teaching Audio Podcast > www.DrRuthTanyi.org/dr-ruth-podcast

BIBLIOGRAPHY

———————————— † ————————————

American Psychiatric Association. Diagnostic and Statistical Manual of Mental Disorders. 5th ed. Washington D.C.: 2013.

https://www.merriam-webster.com

OTHER BOOKS BY DR TANYI

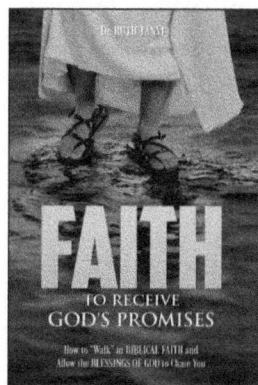

Faith to Receive God's Promises: How to "Walk" in BIBLICAL FAITH and Allow the BLESSINGS OF GOD to Chase You

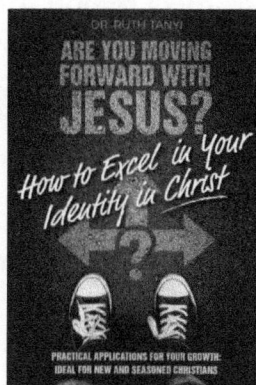

Are You Moving Forward with Jesus? How to Excel in Your Identity in Christ

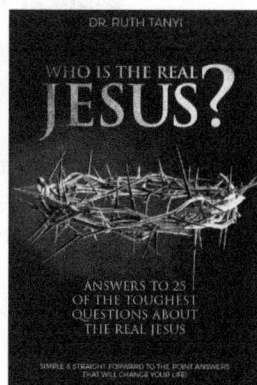

Who is the Real Jesus? Answers to 25 of the Toughest Questions About the Real Jesus.

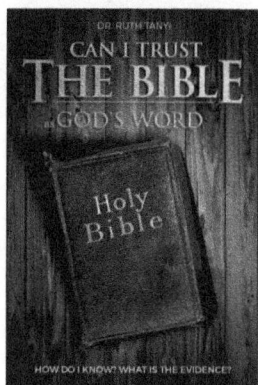

Can I Trust the Bible as God's Word? How Do I know? What is the Evidence?

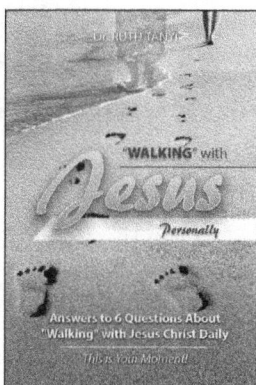

"Walking" with Jesus Personally: Answers to 6 Questions About "Walking" with Jesus Christ Daily: This is Your Moment!

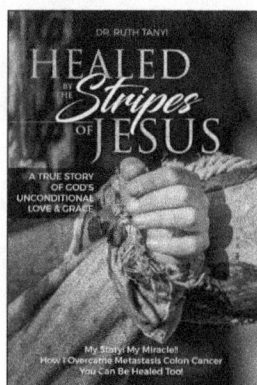

Healed by the Stripes of Jesus: A True Story of God's Unconditional Love and Grace: My Story! My Miracle! How I Overcame Metastasis Colon Cancer: You can Be Healed Too!

MAGAZINES BY DR TANYI

Biblical Preventive Health with Dr Ruth®

- A Magazine by Dr Ruth Tanyi Ministries, Inc.

A Biblical-based Approach to Your Health!

First of its kind Educational Magazine incorporating Biblical Principles and Medical LIfestyle Remedies - Teaching you how to prevent and covercome sicknesses and diseases!

- Approach Your health From a Biblical Perspective
- Foster Overall healing From Within: Mind/Body/Spirit
- Walk in Divine Health - Enjoy Lasting Results

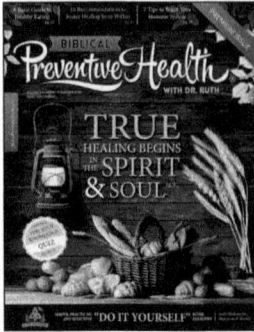

Biblical Preventive Health Magazine:
Volume 1 Number 1:
True Healing Begins in the Spirit & Soul

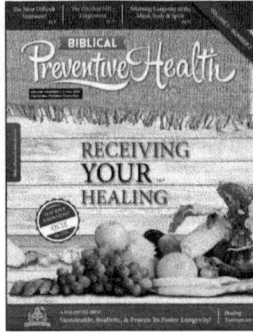

Biblical Preventive Health Magazine:
Volume 1 Number 2:
Receiving Your Healing

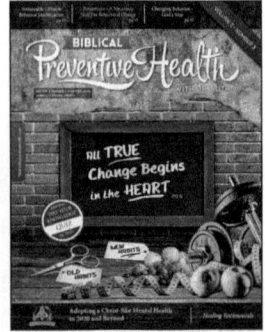

Biblical Preventive Health Magazine:
Volume 2 Number 3:
All True Change Begins in the Heart

Visit our website for more magazine editions

https://www.drruthtanyi.org/biblical-preventive-health-magazine/

USB/AUDIO CD TEACHING LIBRARY

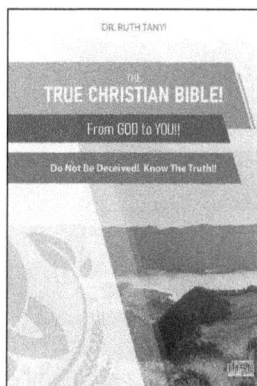

The True Christian Bible!
From God To You!!

Spiritual Warfare: Learn
Practical Ways to Overcome
the Lies from Satan, Your
Past, the Environment, and
Be Set Free in Jesus name!

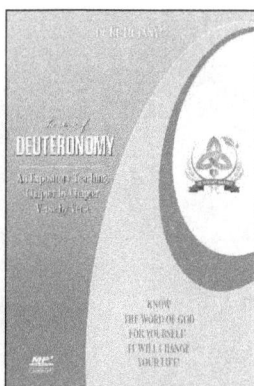

The Book of Deuteronomy:
An Expository Teaching!
Chapter by Chapter, Verse
by Verse

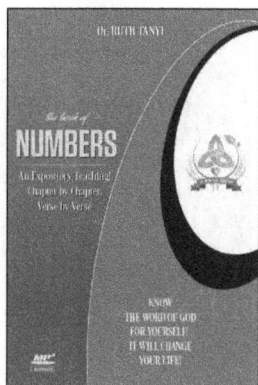

The Book of Numbers: An
Expository Teaching!
Chapter by Chapter, Verse
by Verse

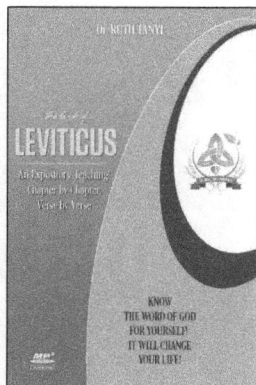

The Book of Leviticus: An
Expository Teaching!
Chapter by Chapter, Verse
by Verse

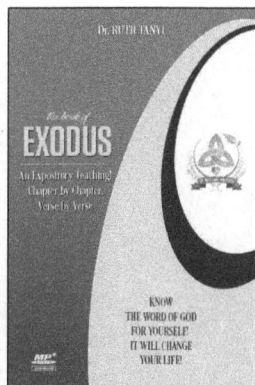

The Book of Exodus: An
Expository Teaching!
Chapter by Chapter, Verse
by Verse

USB/AUDIO CD TEACHING LIBRARY

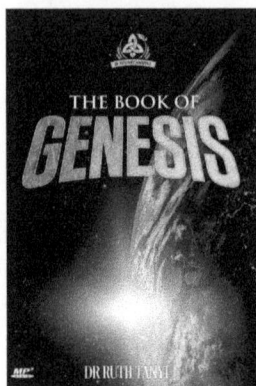

The Book of Genesis: An Expository Teaching! Chapter by Chapter, Verse by Verse

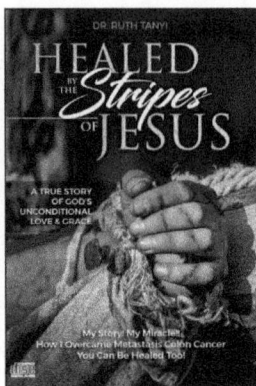

Healed by the Stripes of Jesus: A True Story of God's Unconditional Love and Grace: My Story! My Miracle! How I Overcame Metastasis Colon Cancer: You can Be Healed Too!

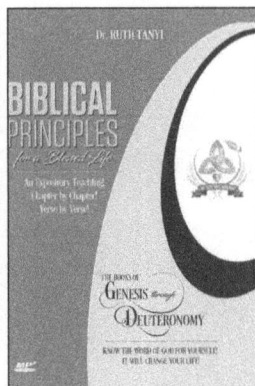

Biblical Principles For a Blessed Life: An Expository Teaching! Chapter by Chapter, Verse by Verse

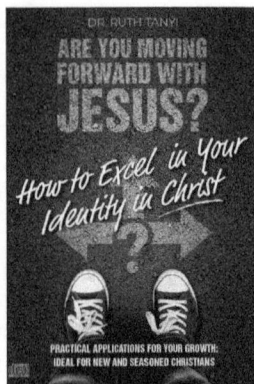

Are You Moving Forward with Jesus? How to Excel in Your Identity in Christ

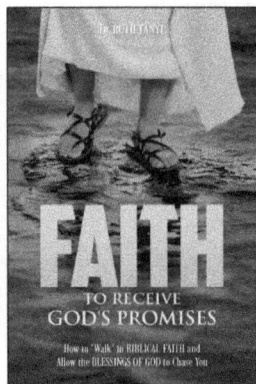

Faith to Receive God's Promises: How to "Walk" in BIBLICAL FAITH and Allow the BESSINGS OF GOD to Chase You

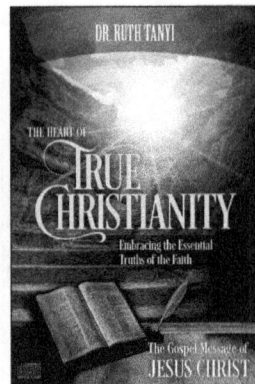

The Heart of True Christianity: Embracing the Essential Truths of the Faith:
The Gospel Message of JESUS CHRIST

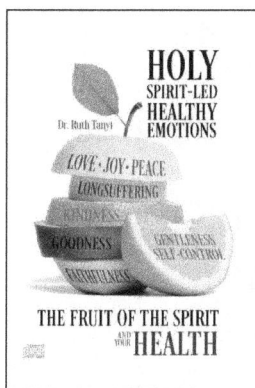

Holy Spirit-Led Healthy Emotions: The Fruit of the Spirit and Your Health

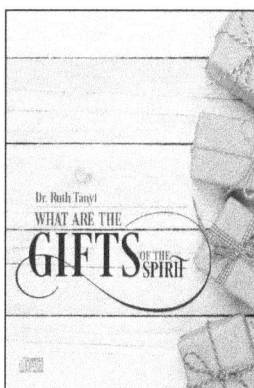

What are the Gifts of the Spirit?

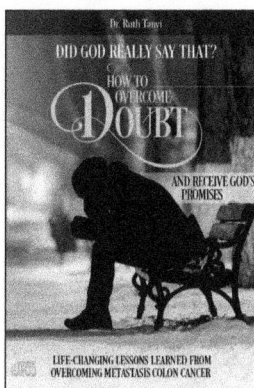

Did God Really Say that: How to Overcome Doubt and Receive God's Promises: Life-Changing Lessons Learned from Overcoming Metastasis Colon Cancer

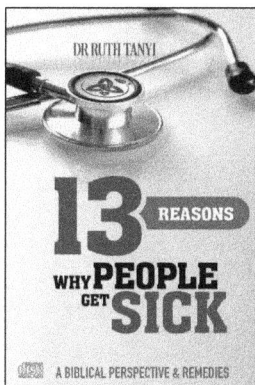

13 Reasons Why People Get Sick: A Biblical Perspective & Remedies

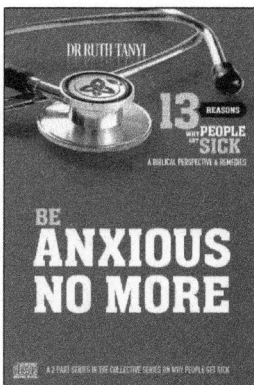

Be Anxious No More: Learn to Overcome Your Anxiety

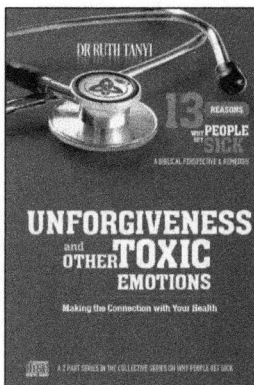

Unforgiveness and Other Toxic Emotions: Making the Connection with Your Health

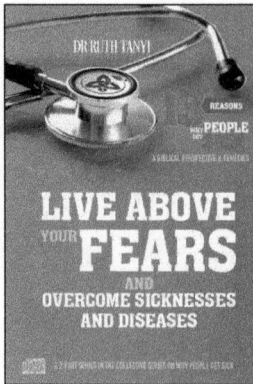

Live Above Your Fears and
Overcome Sicknesses and
Diseases

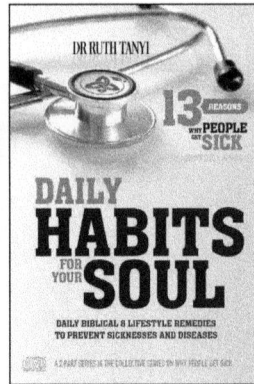

Daily Habits For Your Soul:
Daily Remedies to Prevent
Sicknesses and Diseases

OTHER TEACHINGS BY DR TANYI

Discipleship Bible Teaching Series

Biblical Preventive Health with Dr Ruth ® - A Magazine

13 Reasons Why True Christianity is Different: A Wall Mount Poster

A Call to Action Poster

Visit **Dr Ruth Tanyi Ministries YouTube Channel** and watch our FREE Bible Teachings, Plus Other FREE Devotional Teachings at your convenience, 24/7. Subscribe to our YouTube Channel and start enjoying our Free Teachings Today.

OBTAINING MINISTRY RESOURCES

To get more information about the above ministry resources, please visit our Website: **www.DrRuthTanyi.org**

Contact Information

You can write us at:
Dr Ruth Tanyi Ministries, Inc
P O BOX 1806
Loma Linda, CA, 92354, USA

You Can also Email us at:
Info@DrRuthTanyi.org

ABOUT THE AUTHOR

Dr Ruth Tanyi, DrPH, NP; ACSM HFS; CNS; MA, Ministry

Dr. Ruth Tanyi is a Bible Teacher, Doctor of Preventive Care/Integrative Medicine; Board Certified Nutritionist and Exercise Physiologist; she holds a Master's degree in Ministry. She is the founder/CEO of Dr. Ruth Tanyi Ministries, a non- denominational Christian, non-profit Ministry located in San Bernardino, California, with primary focus on spreading the uncompromising Gospel of Jesus Christ; sharing God's unconditional love and grace, while concurrently teaching others how to integrate Bible-based principles with medical lifestyle practices in order to prevent and overcome diseases.

Even before being healed by God from Metastasis Colon Cancer and other diseases 12 years ago, Dr Ruth felt called by God into Ministry. However, since her healing and experiential knowledge and revelation of the love and grace of God, she has become an ardent student and teacher of the Word of God. Dr Ruth is also actively involved in the Body of Christ via her involvement with other ministries in advancing the Gospel of Jesus Christ, and in espousing the necessity of knowing God's Word. From about 2007 until 2016, Dr Ruth faithfully served as a volunteer at her local church: Abundant Living Family Church (ALFC) in Rancho Cucamonga, California under the leadership of Pastor Diego Mesa; and while there, she counseled and taught individuals about the interconnectedness between God's Word and medical lifestyle practices, and witnessed many transformed lives. She has also served as a Prayer Minister with Andrew Wommack Ministries under the leadership of Andrew Wommack, during his 2016 and 2017 Gospel Truth Conferences, where she ministered and prayed for countless individuals and witnessed their healings and deliverances from all sorts of diseases and bondages.

Dr Ruth's Television appearances as a guest Minister with Fr Mike Manning (deceased) on a series called Catholic Insights, still broadcasting on various Christian TV Networks, continues to educate the public on the major differences between Protestants and Catholics expression of true Christianity. Dr Ruth is a public speaker and author, and offers a CD and DVD teaching library in addition to books on various topics ranging from the essential doctrines of true Christianity, practical application of God's Word in our daily lives, to teachings on the very essential connection between God's Word and Medicine.

Dr Ruth also has a daily Audio Podcast Bible teaching series called **Biblical Principles for a Blessed life**, which is an in-depth teaching across the entire Bible, from the Book of Genesis to Revelation, focusing on teaching others how to practically "live-out" God's Word in their lives. Her practical Bible teachings can also be watched on YouTube (Dr. Ruth Tanyi Ministries, Inc, YouTube Channel), and on Facebook (Dr. Ruth Tanyi Ministries, Inc, Facebook page). You can contact Dr Ruth via Email at DrRuth@DrRuthTanyi.org

www.ingramcontent.com/pod-product-compliance
Lightning Source LLC
LaVergne TN
LVHW041207080426
835508LV00008B/841